Great Lakes Rhythm & Rhyme

Denise Rodgers

illustrated by
Julie Martin

R. River Road Publications, Inc.   830 E. Savidge St., Spring Lake, Michigan 46456

Book ISBN: 0-938682-80-6
CD ISBN: 0-938682-81-4

Text Copyright © 2003, Denise Rodgers
Illustrations © 2003, River Road Publications, Inc.

Printed in the United States of America
Library of Congress Control Number: 2003094925

CONTENTS

MAMMOTH ICE CUBE

Big as Montana
and slow as molasses,
glaciers were ice forms that moved in large masses
staking a path through a part of the earth
digging and melting for all they were worth.

The process was slow – not at all like a quake,
and when it was done, there were five mammoth lakes.
Michigan formed like a mitten or hand.
The U.P* completed the look of the land.
And oh, the Great Lakes, they're our fresh water treasure,
and boating and fishing and swimming's a pleasure.
The next time you're out there and say that it's nice
remember our Great Lakes all started
as ice!

* Upper Peninsula of Michigan

Glaciers formed during the Ice Age. They greatly changed the land and gouged out the Great Lakes.

HOMES

Huron's the lake that begins with an "H."
It's the very first lake in our poem.
It helps to remember the names of the Great Lakes'
first letters spell out the word "HOMES."

Ontario's next – so far off to the east
with a New York and Canada shore.
There's boating and swimming and fishing for salmon
and walleye, and still, there's much more.

Michigan's huge and it's off to the west.
It's Wisconsin's, Chicago's gold coast.
The beaches are sandy on Michigan's side,
(at least that's what people there boast).

Erie is south and it borders on Buffalo,
Cleveland and Canada, too.
Each lake is so vast that there's room for the swimmers,
the boaters, and freighters with crew.

Superior's north and as cold as an ice cube.
It's massive and make no mistake,
it's wider and deeper than all of the others,
the grandest and largest Great Lake!

Imagine a house that's the home of the Great Lakes,
a house filled with great books and poems
to help you remember that all of the Great Lakes'
first letters spell out the word
HOMES!

DRIP DROP

If you were a drop, just a tiny young drip,
and felt it was time that you'd taken a trip,
why, you could head out Lake Superior way.
Just roll through the lake and you'd start on your way.

Superior's highest,
the Great Lakes' high peak.
The truth is Superior has a small leak.
It spills down to Huron
by day and by night,
and also Lake Michigan, both the same height.

These two lakes are huge, and the water is rough.
You'd float and you'd surge,
swim through all kinds of stuff.
You'd come to the point where Lake Huron drops down,
and flow down to Erie, and spin round and round.

But gravity pushes and jostles and calls,
till you'd find your way over Niagara Falls!
Just roaring and churning, so 3-D and stereo,
five hundred feet down to the quiet Ontario.

Then over the currents you'd glide, oh so fast,
a roller-coast ride, you'd be having a blast!
The Saint Lawrence River will give you the notion
that soon you'll be part of the Atlantic Ocean.

From there, head to Europe and don't ever stop.
The world is wide open for one little drop.

EVERY DAY NEW

Glimmering, shimmering, endless and blue,
thrashing and crashing,
it's every day new.

Sometimes it's gray with a glimmer of light.
Sometimes it shines with the full moon at night,
painting the water all yellow and black.
Sunrise comes up and the blueness comes back.
Polishes pebbles and
plays with the sand,
changing the look of the shore and the land.

Howling with grief through a cold, wintry gale,
lapping in summer, so clear and so pale.
Sometimes so sharp, like a streak in the sky,
sometimes so muted, a color gone shy.
Drifts in the winter like scenes from the moon,
melts in the spring sun, but never too soon.
Sunken ship treaures and eerie night ghosts
known for their visits on every lake coast.

So many secrets, so vast and so deep,
secrets that only a Great Lake could keep.

A DOG FOR ALL SEASONS

Some like San Diego
where the weather's always great.
I prefer the seasons
that we have near our Great Lakes.

In winter, when I walk my dog,
it's freezing, but we go.
He sticks his head in snow banks
and his face lifts up the snow.
When spring is here, the leaves sprout forth.
My dog is such a pain.
He dashes out and tromps into
the puddles in the rain.
The summer's warm and humid
and the sun shines hot and bright.
I take my dog out walking
in the coolness of the night.
When autumn comes, we really like
the brisk October breeze.
We crunch the leaves together
as they float down from the trees.

Some like San Diego,
say it has the perfect weather.
But we prefer four seasons –
that's my dog and I together!

GREAT FREIGHTERS

If you live near Great Lakes, then sooner or later you'll sit on the shore and you'll watch a great freighter, chugging and steaming throughout the Great Lakes, pushing the water, with waves in its wake. Some are so huge, at one thousand feet long, filled up with cargo and crew thirty strong. The freighters haul limestone and coal, iron ore. They drop off their cargo and load up some more. Look on the lake when the dark takes the night. The freighters shine out with their sides strung with lights. The Great Lakes are huge and there isn't much greater than going to shore just to watch a great freighter.

NIAGARA CALLS

When I'm stressed,
when nature calls,
I think about
Niagara Falls.
One-fifty thousand
gallons in it
dropping
every
single
minute.
Sounds like
thunder,
trains and more,
or how
ten thousand
lions roar.
When nature calls,
just answer to it.
Skip Niagara –
go and do it!

*Niagara Falls is
one of the largest
(but not highest)
waterfalls in the world.
An island at the top
divides the water into two falls: Horseshoe Fall,
2600 feet wide, and American Fall, 1000 feet wide.*

TAHQUAMENON FALLS

Water rushing,
gushing,
pushing
past the limits of the edge.
Water barrels off the ledge,
whipping up the bottom sludge,
makes the water look like fudge,
growling with a freight train's roar,
wildly rushes out some more.

You could harness all the power
as it flashes hour by hour
and will never, ever stop,
thickly loaded from the top.
Water flowing, swiftly whooshing,
always whisking, always pushing
to the river down below,
always rushing, never slow,
till it falls right past the islands,
gives it just another try and
with a mild and calming quiver,
it becomes a simple river.
It's amazing if you spy it;
all that noise and then the
Quiet.

The Tahquamenon Falls is in the Upper Peninsula of Michigan and is 200 feet wide and drops nearly 50 feet. These falls were the inspiration for Henry Wadsworth Longfellow's poem Hiawatha.

SUMMER COTTAGE

It smells just like mold in our cottage,
and sometimes we know there are mice.
But still, it's our Great Lakes vacation,
so we think our cottage is nice.
We pack all our clothes every weekend,
and then we go driving up north.
By Sunday we're back in the city.
It's fun to go drive back and forth.

The beaches are loaded with pebbles.
Our feet get all coated with sand.
We swim all the way to the sandbar,
and then we stop swimming and stand.
The water is cool and we're floating
on innertubes, rounded and black.
Or sometimes we dive underwater
or float on our stomachs or backs.

When night falls we watch all the freighters
and sit by the fire on the beach.
And everyone's roasting a hot dog,
or eating an apple or peach.
The summer goes fast at our cottage.
When school starts, we close it and then,
by springtime we're happy that winter has passed
and we start it all over again.

MICHIGAN MAP POEM

Saginaw Bay is the crook of a mitten.
Port Hope is right up near the thumb.
Manistee sits right where you'd put your pinky.
The Lansing spot taps on a drum.
Sturgis is south, at the base of the wrist
and there's Mackinac at the tip top.
There are so many cities in Michigan's mitten.
Recite them and you'll never stop.

Mount Pleasant, Ann Arbor and Kalamazoo
Adrian, Midland and Frost,
Alpena, Kalkaska, Boyne City and Bath.
Keep driving until you get lost.

The mitten is grand, it is large it is super,
but down there you'll never get close to a yooper.
A yooper's a person who's from the U.P.*
The part of the state where there's much more to see.
There's Laurium, Skandia, Limestone and Tula,
Marquette, Iron Mountain and Gay.
There's Drummond and White Pine and Greenland
and Johnsville and Witch Lake and Keweenaw Bay.

So go for a ride, get out there exploring
no matter how long it might take.
And if you get finished with finding the cities,
then next you can look for the lakes . . .

* Upper Peninsula of Michigan

LIGHTHOUSE

There once was a man who was scared of the dark.
So he went off to live all alone in a park
by the side of the shore, at the edge of the lake,
and his family was sure he had made a mistake.
For with no city near it would give him a fright
to have only the stars and the moon for his light.
But what they didn't know (and they should have looked deeper),
his job (what a job!) was the new lighthouse keeper.

As soon as the sun looked as if it might set,
he would follow his cue — that it was time to get
up the stairs of the lighthouse to light up the sky.

His relatives learned of his work, by and by.
And they'd come by to visit, but only at night
when he'd climb up the steps,
several stories in height.
He would light up the sky,
for the ships out so far,
brightly shining the way,
like a fiery star.

The light was his light,
and was his light to keep.
(And all through the day
it was his time to sleep.)

THIRSTY GIANT

There once was a giant both thirsty and parched.
He wanted a drink, so he walked and he marched.
He saw the Great Lakes, and he felt very needy.
The problem was that he was also quite greedy.
He sucked down the lakes till he wanted to burst,
so dry was his throat and so strong was his thirst.
He sat by the lake, which had water no more,
and stared at the basin, the rich muddy floor.

He went for a walk for a quick look and see.
The lake, not a lake, just between you and me.
Instead it was craters and mud pocked with boats,
all left on the bottom with no need to float.
He passed a few shipwrecks from days of the past
when ships sailed the lakes with the wind on their mast.
He walked through Lake Erie, and looked for the falls,
said, "Boy, I was thirsty, but I miss it all."
He reached for the clouds, and he grabbed them with pain.
He twisted and twirled them till they spat off rain.
The skies turned all dark and he made a big wish.
"Please fill up the lakes and please save all the fish."

For many a day and for many a night
the water surged down till the lakes were made right.
The clouds gave the giant advice and one tip,
"The next time you're thirsty—just stick with one sip."

HUNTING FOR MASTODON

Imagine going back in time
and going for a hunt.
The mastodon is eight feet tall!
(And that one is a runt.)

He's something like an elephant,
but still, you quash your fears,
as you and other hunters gather
'round him with your spears.

The hunt goes well. You get your kill.
But then your work begins.
You use your kill for food and clothes
– so everybody wins.

You scrape the hide. You spear the meat
and roast it on a pit.
You'd even dry and use the bones.
You wouldn't waste a bit.

Today it's so much easier.
You take your car and park it
and buy your food, your clothes, your shoes
by shopping at the market.

But that is how the shopping went
10,000 years ago.
You'd take your spear, and set your jaw
and off to hunt you'd go.

HUNTING UP NORTH

They liked to do their hunting with
       big antlers on their heads,
wrapped in furs turned inside out
       so they'd be warm instead.

The Great Lakes were all frozen land
       of tundra, spruce and snow.
The hunters lived down in the south
       but they'd pack up and go.

They'd take their antlers, furs and spears,
       and leave their kin behind,
and then go tromping north to hunt
       for all that they could find.

They'd hunt for bison, mastodon
       for mammoth, caribou.
They'd creep up close and throw their spears,
       as able hunters do.

They'd get their kill, and tie it up,
       and then commence to roam,
and wouldn't take their antlers off
       'til they were safely home.

The earliest Great Lakes people came to North America over the Bering Straits land bridge sometime between 14,000 and 11,000 BC. They followed the mammoth, caribou, mastodon and prehistoric bison. Because of the glacial climate, these people hunted the Great Lakes region and returned to warmer land in the south to live.

SWEETWATER SEAS

The French were explorers and they knew their stuff.
They traveled the New World, so rugged and tough.
They came to the Great Lakes and what did they see?
They named these blue waters the "Sweetwater Seas."

Seas to the South, to the North, to the West,
waters and land undeniably blessed.
These "oceans" were different, they knew on the spot.
The water had no salt, not one single drop.

The Sweetwater Seas were so vast to explore.
They rowed on for days without finding a shore.
They knew it was special and made them feel free,
just sailing for days on the Sweetwater Seas.

The Sweetwater Seas are still with us today.
We use them for drinking, for boating and play.
The shores lined with cities, with people, with trees.
We call them the Great Lakes,
our Sweetwater Seas.

THE NORTHWEST PASSAGE

They came here from England, from Spain and from France.
They came for the journey, adventure, romance.
Some took to the Great Lakes, so vast and so wide,
convinced they'd find China beyond the west side.

They searched and explored all the freshwater seas.
But all that they found was the forests and trees,
the natives, the copper, the quartz and the lakes.
The sheer disappointment was too much to take.

Their sadness so keen with the beauty they'd found.
Instead of great pleasure, they fretted and frowned.
So keep this in mind when you're wanting a lot.
Check out what you have—and enjoy what you've got!

*Christopher Columbus came across the Atlantic in 1492
in search of the Far Eastern countries of China and
India. He and the explorers who followed for centuries
were convinced that there was a "Northwest Passage"
waterway that cut through this "New World."*

A BEAVER HAT

A beaver hat.
Imagine that!
Everyone wanted a beaver hat.
From Paris to London
and halfway to Rome
everyone wanted
a hat of their own.

No trapper took possum
or raccoon or deer.
The beaver style lasted
some 300 years!

But as it had started
it came to an end.
There's just no accounting
for this fashion trend.

The trappers lost money,
but make no mistake.
The beavers felt safer
by every Great Lake!

Beaver fur drove the French fur-trapping trade in the Great Lakes region from the early 1500s to the mid-1800s.

FURS TO TRADE

Furs to trade.
Furs to trade.
From the ones who wear a braid.
We have otter, fox and mink.
Beaver is top choice, I think.

We trade for colored cloth and beads,
metal tools for planting seeds,
tools we use to help us cook.
Boiling pot? We'll take a look.
Muskets, guns and hunting knives,
trading's changed our daily lives.

Goods that we once thought were strange,
now we need; they've made us change.
We trade goods; that's how we're paid.
Furs to trade.
Furs to trade.

INDIAN NAMES

The natives had language before white men came.
Their words, filled with large sounds, gave cities their names.
Leelanau's beauty, a gift to the sight,
was Indian language for "Delight of Life."

The islands that both bear the name "Manitou"
carry the meaning "Great Spirit" right through.
"Menominee" rolls off the tongue very nice.
Who knew that its meaning is "country of rice"?

When morning is near and it's night that is done,
think of "Petoskey," which means "rising sun."
Go to Lake Erie and please notice that
the lake is NOT creepy, it's named for a "cat."

Are these too tricky?
Your tongue's in a wrench?
Wait till we bring up the names from the French!

HOW DULUTH GOT ITS NAME

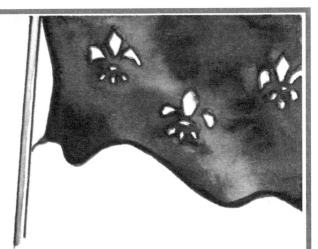

Would you like to know it?
Would you like the truth
of how this fair city
got named as Duluth?

Then fasten your seat belt
pull up your pants.
Duluth got its name from
a trader from France.

When Sieur du Luth claimed
all the land for King Louis,*
the natives thought, "Hold on,
it's our land! P-touie!"

The French took it over
and used it the most.
It grew as the site of
a fur trading post.

It was so remote, yet
it grew just the same.
And that is the truth, how
Duluth got its name.

* In 1679, Sieur du Luth claimed the land at the western end of Lake Superior for King Louis XIV (pronounced "Louie") of France.

BEFORE ALL THE FREIGHTERS

Before all the freighters,
before all the motors,
before all the skiers,
before all the boaters,
before all the steamships,
and sailboats, it's true,
the only good boat
was the sturdy canoe,
of birchbark and wood frame
and resin for glue,
so lightweight, efficient,
swift-gliding for two.

Image the Great Lakes so calm.
Go and try it.
With only canoes as our boats...
oh, how quiet!
You'd hear drops of water.
You'd hear every oar,
the cry of the the seagulls,
the wind's steady roar.

The Great Lakes were quiet.
just different, no greater,
before every steamship,
before every freighter.

GHOST TOWN

In two hotels, they lithely creep.
The ghostly tourists come to sleep.
And now, shut down, forever still
are two, once-bustling lumber mills.
The pub, the band and so much more,
at least one well-stocked general store.

A city, once so proud and cocky,
like Chicago or Milwaukee.
Now quiet,
hushed,
and filled with sand
beneath the surface, once so grand.

No songs, no schools, no talk, no sport,
though once it was a Great Lake port.
It was a town that lost its luck,
a town just south of Saugatuck.
And now it's sunk beneath the shore,
the ghostly town of Singapore.

One of Michigan's most famous ghost towns, Singapore, was founded in the 1830s by New York land speculators. The western Michigan city thrived as a busy lumbering town until the 1870s, when the supply of lumber ran out.

GHOST SHIPS

The storms and the winds of the Great Lakes are deadly
and ships have been lost in the gales.
And though all may sink to the depth of the lakebed,
some say they can still hear the wails.

Appearing in mists and the fog of the night as
they never will venture by day,
the ghosts of the lake prefer shadows and darkness
as that is their charge and their way.

It's ghostly, it's ghoulish,
if just a bit foolish
to search for these sailors at noon.
The ghost ships take charge
in the cover of darkness
and sail by the light of the moon.

The waters are haunted,
but here is a promise:
you'll not find one ghost by mistake.
The men of the ghost ships won't
haunt your warm bedroom;
they only appear on the lake.

ERIE CANAL

Bridges of water and boats pulled by mules,
the Erie Canal went and broke all the rules
by winding across New York State like a snake,
connecting the Hudson to Erie's Great Lake.

They dug with their hands and they built it with pride,
with four feet of depth and just forty feet wide.
The settlers rode west at just four miles an hour.
(It's hard to go fast when a mule is the power.)

But so many came for a new life "out west,"
that thousands of settlers joined with the rest.
The farms near the lakes shipped their food to the east
and gave the New Yorkers a new Midwest feast,
by selling their corn crop, and apples and cherries,
and shipping off all that the barges could carry.

The Erie Canal was for much more than show.
It helped the Great Lakes and America grow.
But then came the railroads and roads as we see 'em,
all making the Erie Canal a museum.

It's part of our history, part of our past.
(Today when we travel, we like to go fast!)

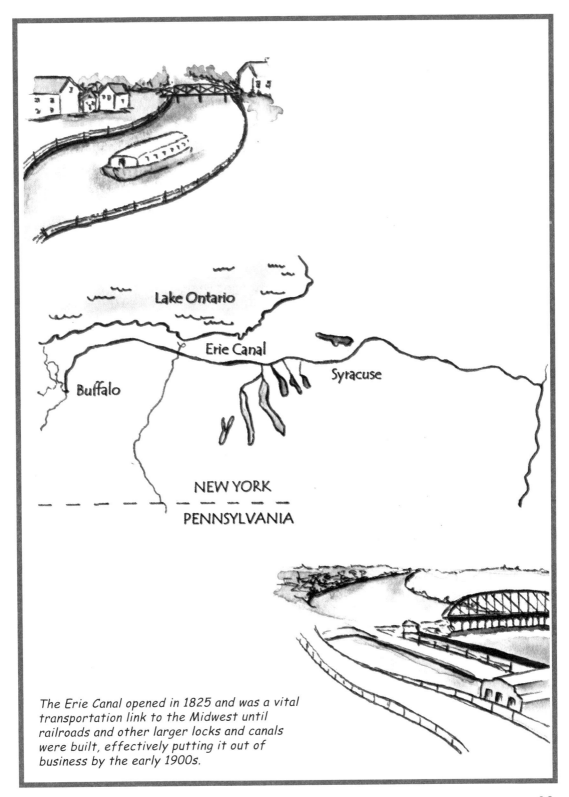

Lake Ontario

Erie Canal

Buffalo

Syracuse

NEW YORK

PENNSYLVANIA

The Erie Canal opened in 1825 and was a vital transportation link to the Midwest until railroads and other larger locks and canals were built, effectively putting it out of business by the early 1900s.

CAPTAIN FISH & WALK-IN-THE-WATER

This tale is the tale of a man, Captain Fish.
Commanding a ship was his one special wish.
In 1818, he set off on a trip
with "Walk-in-the-Water," a wood-burning ship.

The first of its kind, with both sidewheel and steam,
it chugged through the water like some kind of dream.
Not one other ship was alike or the same.
The natives, amused, quickly gave it its name.

Just three short years later, on Halloween night,
the crew and their guests had a terrible fright.
A storm wrecked the ship; it was battered and tossed.
The crew saved the passengers; not one was lost.

This steamship with masts is a memory now,
a part of Lake Erie, its stern to its bow.
The Walk-in-the-Water, the dream and the wish,
of one Great Lakes mariner, one Captain Fish.

WHALEBACKS

Did you know?
Could you know?
If this is true...
a long ago time in the deep water blue,
that whales sailed the lakes to the oceans and back,
but not real live whales, but a ship with a back.

The ships with a back called the "whalebacks" were rare,
but there was a time when they sailed everywhere.
Superior waters saw whalebacks and then,
they'd sail down to Erie and back up again.

The whalebacks were sturdy and rounded and stout.
They looked much like whales, yet had no kind of spout.
They carted the big loads and people, it's true,
out sailing the Great Lakes, the big, vast, deep blue.

THE WHITE-TAIL CAFÉ

Welcome, my deer,
　　　　to the White-Tail Café.
Because it is summer
　　　　our menu today
has mushrooms, tomatoes
　　　　and wildflower stew,
some tasty young carrots
　　　　we've plucked just for you.

So glad it's not winter
　　　　when food is so stark
that all we can offer
　　　　is four kinds of bark,
from maple and birch to
　　　　some willow or oak.
Well, that's what we serve to
　　　　our deerly loved folk.

It's more than a buck, but
　　　　we hope that you'll stay
for not that much doe at
　　　　the White-Tail Café.

MEETING MOOSE

On Isle Royale, there's no excuse
for missing out on meeting moose
or wolves or loons, a jay or fox.
You'll likely meet them, and if not
you won't find temple, church or steeple.
Really, there's not many people,
just trees and bogs and inland lakes.
So drift on through, make no mistake.
It's fun to wander on the loose.
So take a hike and
meet some moose.

PORCUPINE

The thing about the porcupine –
he has no pork. He has no pine.
He does have quills, these long thin spikes
that no one but the porc'-pine likes.
He'll use them when he's in a mood.
(Like when you're loud or mean or rude.)
They won't feel good. They'll make you pout.
They go in quick. They won't come out.
So if a porcupine is present,
make sure that you are nice and pleasant.

FAREWELL TO FISHFLIES

They land in your hair.
They cover the chair.
They fly in your face,
all over the place.
They cover the tree.
They're all over me.
You step, they go crunch.
But I have a hunch
that they'll go away.
They last just one day.
You won't see me cry.
I'll just say,
"Bye, bye."

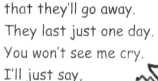

FIREFLIES

If you're out by the lake
and the stars seem too close
and they twinkle and stop
like you've just seen a ghost,
please don't run to your mama
and ask for a hug.
Because that's not a star,
or a ghost . . .
It's a bug!

So get out your jar,
punch some holes,
bring a net,
as a firefly makes
an enlightening pet.

Also known as mayflies, fishflies swarm the shores of the Great Lakes in June, providing an abundant food source for bats, fish and birds. While they live for two years as larva, they fortunately live for just twelve hours as adults—unable to eat or bite as they have no mouths.

ZEBRA MUSSEL

The zebra mussel is a snot
that no one really likes a lot.
It's not a zebra,
not a horse.
It's not a muscle man, of course.

Instead a mollusk with a shell
and zebra stripes
so you can tell
(in case you have a test or quiz)
just what a zebra mussel is.

They hog the plankton.
They don't care,
and never, ever, ever share.
They stick to valves, to pipes and ships.
They latch on tight; they hold their grip
and never think of letting go.
Don't think to ask; they'd just say, "NO!"

They only came here by mistake.
I'd like them out of each Great Lake.
They are a stain,
a pain,
a blot.
The zebra mussel is a snot.

Zebra mussels are not native to the Great Lakes but probably came here in the ballast water of ships traveling into the Great Lakes from the ocean.

ROBIN RED BREAST

Turdus migratorius, a Great Lakes favorite bird,
is known as "robin red breast" with a different choice of words.
When you hear the Latin name, it makes you think of turds.

Now this could be an awful sight,
a yicky, sticky splotch of white.

Instead imagine her in flight
with wings of gray and breast orange-red,
a treetop nest her simple bed,
with worms that make her feel well fed.
Ugh!

Okay,
instead imagine that it's fall.
In order to escape it all,
she's flying south to have a ball.

And when she's done with winter's fling,
you'll find her flying north in spring,
her orange breast flying with gray wings.
She cuts through air and flies with grace,
just pointing with her small gray face
back to the Lakes, her favorite place.

It really is so glorious
to see her glide and soar-ious,
that "Turdus migratorius."

Turdus migratorius, or the robin, is the state bird of Michigan and Wisconsin.

THE COMMON LOON

If you should hear the common loon,
she sings a sad, uncommon tune.
She sings the most from May till June.

The tremolo, her crazy laugh,
a quick hello, while on her path,
or sometimes, it's a sound of wrath.

And don't forget her haunting wail.
She sings this song to find her male,
a song so true it cannot fail.

And there's the one-note, family "hoo."
The mother loon calls, "Where are you?
Get over here right now! One – two!"

The male will yodel for his space.
He'll yodel at another face
until it leaves without a trace.

The common loon's a water fowl
that heads straight south for warmth in fall.
A loony choice?
No, not at all.

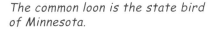

*The common loon is the state bird
of Minnesota.*

FOR THE BIRDS

If you should go birding
        on Saginaw Bay,
you must pack your gear for
        an extra-long day.

So bring your binoculars.
        If you're in luck,
you might get a look at
        a harlequin duck.

And step very carefully.
        You may find soon
that you're face-to-face with
        a red-throated loon.

And making their way through
the wetlands and ponds
are great white-fronted geese and
some trumpeter swans.

Just hike though the marshland
        and it might be pleasant
to spy through your glasses
        just one ring-necked pheasant.

So, go have some fun!
        If you do, take my word
that birding all day's simply
        not for the birds.

SWAMP

A swamp, a fen, a marsh, a bog;
they're all the same.
You trudge, you slog.
The ground is soft and wet and spongy.
Just stay a while and you'll feel grungy.
And walk a little further yet.
Your feet sink in;
your legs are wet.
Stay long enough,
you very might
be getting a mosquito bite.

There's dogfish, cattails,
frogs and otters,
some turtles, beavers in the water,
some hawks and ducks and northern pike,
bald eagles, black birds –
much to like.
So grab your boots and come on in.
It's better if you do not swim,
but save the wetlands
marsh and bogs
for all the turtles
ducks and frogs.

APPLE PICKING

The air is crisper than the apples
that go crunch.
They hang so heavy on the trees and
I've a hunch
that apples simply wait their turn
for getting eaten.
No need for sugar, cinnamon,
or to be sweetened.

So eat your Empire, Gala,
Northern Spy, Ida Red,
or chomp on juicy Macintosh
or Fugi instead.
The trees all smell of apple
and of blue sky and fall.
My basket's grown so heavy
I can't carry it all.
There's ten gigantic Granny Smith
and one dozen Rome.
I guess I'll just keep eating
them the whole way home.

Apples are an important crop along the Great Lakes in Wisconsin, Michigan, and New York, and Ontario, Canada.

AUTUMN CORN

Corn on the stalk is so sturdy to stand.
Corn set in rows neatly cover the land.
Plucked from their stalks
and then stacked where they park it,
loaded on trucks and then sent out to market.

Corn perched on shelves in the grocery store,
packed up and stacked up from ceiling to floor.
Pulled from the shelves, neatly placed in a cart.
Off to the checkout and then the fun starts.
Corn boiled in pans till the water runs yellow.
Biting so crunchy, its taste sweet, but mellow.

It's been my favorite, since I was born,
salted up, buttered up, early fall corn.

EASTERN MARKET

"A dozen for a dollar!"
just hear the peddler holler.
"'Tatoes!
Onions!
Cukes and beets!
Get your Eastern Market meats!"

Walking through an open stall,
air as crisp as early fall.
Not a single business suit,
men in aprons selling fruit.
Smells of cherries fill the air
at this open, daily fair.

Bite an apple, from the start,
taste the juice that's sweet and tart.
Grapes, tomatoes, Bartlett pears,
corn, zucchini, all his wares.

Loaded wagon, boxes, carts
set to go when daylight starts.

Lots of people, such a crowd,
always talking, moving, loud.
Tulips, daisies, phlox and roses,
pushing babies, running noses.
Shopping, talking, scraping feet.
Can't wait,
we'll be back next week.

Eastern Market is in Detroit, Michigan.

COLD CEREAL

A long time ago, with a pan and a pot,
our breakfasts were cooked and they always were hot.
The pancakes and grits and the hot buttered toast,
the bacon, the oatmeal, creamed wheat and French toast.

But then came a thought, which was bold and imperial.
The thought that arrived was the cold breakfast cereal.
The cornflakes and bran flakes and oat-O's and crunchies
made breakfast a time for the crisp and cold munchies.
Just pour on some milk, get a spoon, start to eat.
No cooking at all for a breakfast complete.

The kids loved the change and the dads liked it too.
The moms had less work, so they loved it, it's true.
Inventors? The men who had banished the toast?
W.K. Kellogg and C.W. Post.

In the early 1900s, W.K. Kellogg and C.W. Post turned the town of Battle Creek, Michigan, into the cereal capital of the world with the invention of boxed, cold breakfast cereals.

DARK AND DEEP ~
THE BRAVERY OF MINERS

Deep in the earth
and so far below,
a cave underground
is a dark place to go.

Far from the sun,
without any trace,
you can't see fingers
in front of your face.

Darker than dark,
and blacker than black,
you must have a light
just to find your way back.

Miners went down
with picks and an ax,
for light, one thick wick
in a candle of wax.

Down in the dark,
the deepest black cave.
The miners were tough,
undeniably
brave.

KABOOM!

Kaboom!
Ka-blast!
Way in the past
the miners mined for ore.
They searched for copper, iron and salt,
for that and much, much more.

Kaboom!
The bite
of dynamite
cut deep inside the earth.
The charge explodes revealing lodes
of minerals of worth.

Kaboom!
The dust,
the air so mussed
went swirling to the sky.
It was a sight, the dynamite
that made the mountains fly.

Kaboom!
The earth
was filled with mirth
so tickled by the boom.
The miner's pleasure,
each newfound treasure
that followed each
Kaboom!

Mining is an important part of the Great Lakes' past.

IN PAUL BUNYAN'S TIME

In Paul Bunyan's time
when this giant made tracks ...
most Great Lakes pine trees
were felled by the ax.
Lumberjacks came and cut
so many down,
chopping the pines
to make wood to build towns.

Their work was important;
they did what they should,
out filling the need
of our country for wood.
It's different today.
As we leave trees behind
and also plant new trees.

It's good to be kind
to the squirrels, the raccoons,
and the owls and deer,
the wildlife we see
and to those we just hear.

A trek through the woods,
through the hush of white pine
reminds us of when
it was Paul Bunyan's time.

The timber boom of the last half of the 1800s generated millions of dollars and employed thousands of lumberjacks. Concern over the way that the cleared land was left behind led to conservation programs that are still in effect today.

THE LUMBERJACKS' SONG

Imagine the forest with pine trees so high,
so lush and so thick that they covered the sky.
Imagine your job–that you carried an ax
wore flannels and jeans–you're a strong lumberjack.

The lumberjack's strong and the lumberjack's limber.
The lumberjacks called out, "It's falling–oh, TIMBER!"

Imagine your days spent with sawing and chopping
and felling the pine trees with no thought of stopping.
Just working so hard with your strength and your might,
working all day till the day turns to night.
Refrain

The cook and the "cookee" make three meals a day.
Your work day's so long, there's not much time for play.
You eat meals in silence–an unwritten rule
with no chance for fighting–just fill up with fuel.
Refrain

Imagine the nights in the winter so long,
no TV or games–but the stories and songs!
You sit by the campfire and warm your cold socks
and sing of Paul Bunyan and Babe, his blue ox.
Refrain

You sleep hard all night 'cause you work hard all day.
You wake up for breakfast and get on your way.
You chow down on pancakes, potatoes, sowbellies,
and cookies and doughnuts and fresh rolls and jellies.
Refrain

UNDERGROUND RAILROAD

A ticket to ride
      on a train underground.
A ticket to ride
      on a train never found.
Take the trip north;
      just pack nothing and flee,
leaving it all
      for the chance to be free.
Hiding in cellars,
      in barns overnight,
living in danger
      and sleeping in fright.
Think of it clearly,
      and you will agree,
the sky is much bluer
      to eyes that are free.

For many years, slaves escaped from the South by following the "Underground Railroad," a series of secret routes and safe houses leading to freedom in the Great Lakes states and Canada.

HENRY FORD

A Great Lakes man named Henry Ford
made lots of cars all could afford,
and paid real well for factory work
to every linesman, hand and clerk.

He set up an assembly line
and every worker did assign
to fit the engines, and each chass
shine each car till it looked brass
tighten screws, install each seat.
Each car became a major feat.

His masterpiece, the Model T,
inspired a major shopping spree,
with fifteen million models made
all on the road, both bought and paid.
It changed the country, such a plan
all from this striving Great Lakes man.

SOO LOCKS

Superior, the highest lake—
when ships would leave it they would break
when passing through the rough St. Marys—
rapids there were wild and scary.
Ships would have to moor and stop
and traverse down the steepest drop.
They'd carry all their cargo then
until they reached the lake again.
And even harder yet to tote
was every heavy, wooden boat.

But then wise people built the locks,
each water-tight convenient box
for every passing boat and ship
just trying to go on a trip.
Each lock's a chamber, water tight,
that lifts the ships as if they're light.
The water fills and ships can rise,
but that's not all the lock's comprise.
They turn a valve and empty out.
That's what the locks are all about.
A ship will drop and pass on through
the famous locks they call the Soo.

The Soo Locks were built in 1855 to lower and raise boats twenty feet from Lake Superior through the St. Marys River, which connects Lake Superior to Lake Huron.

LOCKED UP FOR WINTER

The Great Lakes are north lakes
so we pay the price.
For three months of twelve –
all the locks close for ice.
The locks are like steps,
take the ships up or down
avoiding the rapids, the falls,
and the ground.

The ships carry huge loads
of copper and ore
and gypsum and salt piles
and iron and more.
So all through the spring time,
the summer and fall,
the locks lift the ships
or they lower them all.

But winter is frigid,
It bears saying twice,
the locks are all closed
when they're covered with ice.

PAINTING MIGHTY MAC

My job is a painter.
I paint Mighty Mac.
And, yes, it's a tough job, but I have the knack.
It takes sixty thousand big paint cans or more.
That's more than you'll find at your corner paint store.

Just look at the bridge–about five miles long,
with two-foot-thick cables to make it all strong.
I hang in a basket, five hundred feet high.
The lake swirls below,
and I'm up in the sky.
The winter's so harsh that we don't work at all,
but work from mid-April till it's early fall.

It's nearly ten years till we're finished and then
we buy some more paint and
start over again.

The mighty Mackinac Bridge connects the Upper
and Lower Peninsulas of Michigan. It stretches
about five miles across the Straits of Mackinac.

LAKE EFFECT

Humidity, humidity,
I think it's sheer stupidity.
When it gets cold, you feel the chill.
When warm outside, it's hotter still.
The lake effect brings cloudy days.
They make the sky a coat of grays.

There's also much more rain and snow.
It helps the vegetation grow.
But when the lake is somewhat warm
it helps create a nasty storm.
The colder air atop the lake
will whip around and start to make
a whopping, heaping load of white,
a fluffy, puffy, winter sight.

So, if you say this, you're correct:
"It's all a part of
lake effect."

*The Great Lakes greatly affect the weather
in the states that border them.*

MOTOWN USA

In the heart of Detroit, far away from L.A.,
a music sound grew that still lives to this day.
The hippest, the wildest, the best of its time.
The critics all loved it and called it sublime.
The teenagers danced and they rocked all around.
The music they loved was the new Motown sound.

The fans sang along.
Some would shout.
Some would scream,
or they'd dance right along with the Tops or Supremes,
Martha Reeves, Little Richard,
years later, for action
they'd walk on the moon with pop king Michael Jackson.
There's Smokey and Stevie, and then the Temptations.
They all changed the sound of hit tunes 'round the nation.

"I heard through the grapevine"
"Oh postman, oh please"
or "I'll shop around
like my mama told me,"
the frug and the jerk* and the "tears of a clown"
became a big part of the old Motown sound.

* The frug (pronounced "froog") and the jerk were dances popular during the
late 1960s.

55

GREAT LAKES RHYTHM AND RHYME

The Great Lakes are great lakes
for rhythm and rhyme.
They shimmer and shimmy
in three-metered time.
They bathe us in blueness,
their summer sand warm.
They've eaten up freighters
and ships in a storm.

They guide us, they quench us with legends and tales,
the stories of natives and old settlers' trails.
They etch out a land, on the maps where it's written,
and carve out a shape that resembles a mitten.

They're teeming with sand dunes,
with hunters for sport,
surrounded by state parks
and these major ports:
Buffalo, Erie, Toronto, Marquette,
Chicago, Milwaukee, Detroit,
and more yet.

They're vast like the oceans, connected by straits.
They're wondrous, they're endless,
the rhythmic Great Lakes.

INDEX

ACKNOWLEDGEMENTS

With special thanks...

To reference librarians everywhere for the wonderful work you do!

To proofreaders/nitpickers extraordinaire, Doris Schey and Shelly Lazarus.

To Julie Martin for adding a third, fourth, and fifth dimension to this project with her art.

To David Rodgers for helping me hear the beat.

To Peter, Ted, David, and my parents for their everlasting support.

To Lynne and the wonderful crew at River Road for making it all happen.

Denise Rodgers

A big thanks to the following:

Once again to Denise Rodgers. It's always fun.

Also thanks to all at River Road Publications. It has been a pleasure working with you.

To my family, who put up with the sandwiches and the fast food while mom paints.

And to my mom and dad, who are becoming quite the marketing and P.R. experts.

Julie Martin

WHO CAME UP WITH THIS BOOK?

The Poet

Denise Rodgers is a poet and professional writer whose head is full of rhymes (she can't stop them). Some of these have found their way to publications such as *Children's Digest*, *Junior Trails*, and Jack Prelutsky's *The 20th Century Collection of Poetry for Children*. Lots of others can be found in her first book, *A Little Bit of Nonsense*.

Although she is called "The Poetry Lady" by those familiar with her poems and poetry workshops, Denise also writes advertising, news columns, and features for businesses. She lives with her husband and sons (when they are home from college) in Huntington Woods, Michigan. The family especially enjoys weekends at their Lake Huron cottage.

The Illustrator

Julie Martin is an artist whose pen tends to get wild and wacky after she reads The Poetry Lady's verses. Fortunately, Julie has a serious day job in the corporate world and a husband and two sons in Shelby Township, Michigan, to help keep her grounded. Her delightful art can also be found in the first Rodgers book, *A Little Bit of Nonsense*.